DRUGS & CONSEQUENCES™

THE TRUTH ABOUT
HEROIN

PHILIP WOLNY

ROSEN
PUBLISHING®

New York

Published in 2014 by The Rosen Publishing Group, Inc.
29 East 21st Street, New York, NY 10010

Library of Congress Cataloging-in-Publication Data

Wolny, Philip.
The truth about heroin/Philip Wolny.—First edition.
    pages cm—(Drugs & consequences)
Includes bibliographical references and index.
ISBN 978-1-4777-1898-8 (library binding)
1. Heroin—Juvenile literature. 2. Heroin abuse—Juvenile literature. I. Title.
RM666.H35W65 2013
616.86'32—dc23

                                                                2013013766

Manufactured in the United States of America

CPSIA Compliance Information: Batch #W14YA: For further information, contact Rosen Publishing, New York, New York, at 1-800-237-9932.

CONTENTS

INTRODUCTION **4**

CHAPTER 1 HEROIN THEN AND NOW **7**

CHAPTER 2 YOUR BRAIN AND BODY ON HEROIN **15**

CHAPTER 3 HEROIN AND HEALTH: THE UGLY TRUTH **26**

CHAPTER 4 THE SO-CALLED LIFE OF AN ADDICT **38**

CHAPTER 5 GETTING CLEAN **46**

GLOSSARY **58**

FOR MORE INFORMATION **59**

FOR FURTHER READING **61**

BIBLIOGRAPHY **62**

INDEX **63**

INTRODUCTION

In early 2013, troubling reports were coming in from all over the United States. Medical first responders and emergency room staff saw the devastating effects firsthand. Calls for ambulances and emergency room visits were rising dramatically. Crimes like burglary and theft were, too. Dozens of state and local governments were declaring medical emergencies. The culprit was one of the most addictive drugs around: heroin.

The heroin epidemic afflicting communities nationwide surprised law enforcement, politicians, and everyday citizens. One long-standing and incorrect myth has been that heroin is a problem limited to major cities. By the late-2000s, heroin's presence in suburbs and small towns could not be ignored. Even more disturbing was the drug's increasing popularity among younger users, including teens.

Jerry Elsner of the Illinois State Crime Commission told the *Chicago Daily Herald* in March 2013 about the more than three thousand heroin overdoses in his state in 2012, adding, "It is an emergency. We could lose a whole generation of kids." Elsner's sentiments were echoed by Risa Vetri Ferman, a district attorney in Montgomery County, Pennsylvania, who told the *Mercury* newspaper, "Years ago you would think about a heroin addict as a junkie…some older person who is

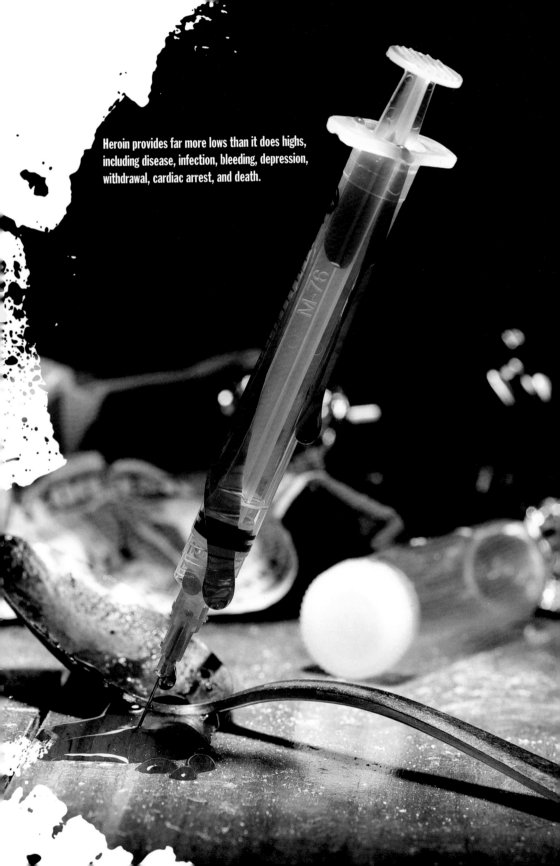

Heroin provides far more lows than it does highs, including disease, infection, bleeding, depression, withdrawal, cardiac arrest, and death.

addicted to this and they're kind of wandering around, out of it all the time. Now we're just seeing a different kind of customer, younger and not necessarily aware of the dangers."

Similar stories have been unfolding in Massachusetts, Missouri, Ohio, Oregon, and many other states. Public health experts and law enforcement agencies blame a combination of factors. A new generation of users is graduating from abusing prescription painkillers and other pharmaceuticals. Heroin is now cheaper than ever, and criminal organizations such as Mexican drug cartels have introduced incredibly potent heroin into thousands of communities.

Along with the deaths caused by overdose, heroin addiction affects the social fabric of communities and can tear families apart. Its victims are often helpless in controlling their behavior because of the drug's power. HIV, hepatitis C, and other diseases that are spread through the use of needles are on the rise, too.

Many people who become heroin addicts think, "It could never happen to me." This is a dangerous myth because the drug can take over the lives of even first-time or casual users. Heroin changes the brain and has many negative effects on a user's health. Addiction makes slaves of heroin users and often leads to a life of sickness, crime, and regret. Addicts risk sacrificing every-thing they cherish in their lives for the drug, receiving jail time for drug-related offenses, and losing their own lives in the process. Discovering how the drug functions in the brain and body of a user, and how addiction regularly devastates the lives it touches, can help one make the right decision to avoid heroin at all costs.

CHAPTER 1

HEROIN
THEN AND NOW

Heroin has been around in many forms for decades. Its narcotic ancestor, opium, appeared in ancient and modern civilizations. Some say it even existed before recorded history. It is part of the class of drugs known as opioids.

Many opioids, but not all, are synthesized from the opium poppy plant. Opium poppies grow in Asian nations such as Afghanistan, Turkey, and Laos, and in the Western Hemisphere in South America and Mexico. Opiates include drugs that are

Outside Kandahar, Afghanistan, poppy farmer Abdul Samad slices opium poppies. Afghanistan remains a major source of heroin, helping feed the addictions of users worldwide, including those in the United States.

naturally derived from the poppy, while opioids include opiates as well as artificial or synthetic versions.

Heroin Emerges

For centuries, the main opiate used worldwide was opium, a paste made from the opium poppy that contains morphine, which itself is used to create heroin. Opium was smoked or otherwise ingested to relieve pain during surgery by ancient Sumerians, Egyptians, Greeks, and Arabs, among others.

The Swiss-German alchemist Paracelsus created laudanum in the sixteenth century, mixing opium, alcohol, and spices as a pain remedy. For centuries, similar painkillers were used to calm down children, cure insomnia, and alleviate the symptoms of dozens of diseases. Many different medications and herbal remedies used opium, and their use in the United States was widespread throughout the nineteenth century.

In 1874, the English chemist and physicist Charles Romley Alder Wright was the first person to synthesize heroin as we know it today. The German chemical and pharmaceutical company Bayer began selling it in 1898 as a pain reliever and cough suppressant. Named after the German word *heroisch*, meaning "powerful," heroin began as a brand-name medicine. "Heroin" was the commercial trademark for the drug's scientific name (diacetylmorphine).

Those who are addicted to heroin are sometimes called "junkies." This is a slang term believed to arise from users at the beginning of the twentieth century who collected scrap metal and other "junk" to pay for their drugs. In the same manner, "junk" sometimes refers to heroin itself.

Back on the Map

Heroin use rises and falls every decade, but the drug always seems to come back. In the 1970s and early 1980s, even strong

THE POPPY AND GEOPOLITICS

Poppy cultivation and the drug trade it supplies have long posed problems in international politics. The British Empire fought the First Opium War (1839–1842) partly to continue importing opium into China, which had tried to ban it and was eventually defeated. Later, Britain and France united for the Second Opium War (1856–1860) to continue to ensure this lucrative trade.

More recently, during the war in Afghanistan that began in 2001, the United States and its military allies have been accused of protecting poppy cultivation. The nation's poppy crop is said to be the world's largest. Critics say this helps fund the warlords allied to Western troops, even though official U.S. policy is aggressively anti-drug. American troops have destroyed poppy fields controlled by its enemies, the Taliban.

samples of heroin were only around 10 percent pure. By the late 2000s, a new heroin epidemic was raging. Mexican drug cartels began importing extremely potent heroin to American streets. Pure heroin can range in color from white to brown, while the Mexican "black tar" variety is among the most potent. It can be sticky, like tar used in roofing, or hard and coal-like, ranging in color from dark brown to black.

Law enforcement and health officials blame the spread of this stronger heroin for rising addiction and overdose rates. Purity levels rose to 35, 50, and even 80 and 90 percent in some

"Black tar" heroin is shown in a close-up. Several types of heroin dominate the North American market, especially this potent strain, mainly originating in Mexico.

regions. Heroin has also become much cheaper as it has become purer and more potent. Most troubling for the authorities has been a newer demographic embracing it: teenagers. For decades, heroin had been associated with urban problems. Throughout the 1990s and the 2000s, however, suburban and rural use exploded.

Rising purity and dropping prices mean that while users once had to shoot up (inject the drug intravenously using needles) for the greatest possible sensation, modern users can smoke or snort heroin and still achieve powerful highs. In areas where the price of a bag of heroin used to be $20, the drug can now be obtained for $10 or even less. This has made it far more affordable for and tempting to teens.

Younger and less experienced users are typically more afraid of needles than hardcore and longtime addicts. Smoking or snorting heroin allows teens to better hide their drug use, since there are no track marks (the scarring made by hypodermic needles) to hide. It also reduces their anxiety about contracting HIV and other blood-borne diseases common to needle users. Psychologically, snorting and smoking heroin can also fool teens into thinking that the drug is somehow safer, when it is anything but.

Graduating from Painkillers

The war on other drugs has had unintended consequences for heroin use. In the 2000s, mainstream use of legal prescription painkillers and other pharmaceuticals skyrocketed. Teens suddenly had much easier access to powerful drugs like oxycodone (brand name: Oxycontin). Even perfectly legal consumers of these drugs abused them. Or their family members gained access to the prescription medicines and used them inappropriately. As a result, illegal, recreational use reached epidemic levels.

Pharmaceutical manufacturers fought back against the abuse of their medicines by changing the drug chemistry. They produced newer versions of oxycodone as time-release painkillers so that users could not get immediate highs through ingestion or by snorting crushed-up pills. Law enforcement and the pharmaceutical industry aggressively teamed up to close "pill mills"—businesses illegally selling prescription pills. The supply of the drugs began to shrink.

Consequently, prescription painkillers became more expensive and, therefore, less desirable. With supplies of painkillers drying up and being priced out of reach, teen users in particular have turned to a drug that provides nearly the same high and is relatively easy to get, potent, and cheaper than ever: heroin.

Overdoses on the Rise

With the increase in consumption of increasingly pure forms of the drug, heroin overdoses are also rising, especially among new and inexperienced users. Even hardcore addicts may encounter extremely pure batches and take too much, resulting in tragedy. As use increases among teens, more of them are moving on to needles, too. Like prescription pill addicts, even users of cocaine and methamphetamine have been switching to heroin because it is more affordable and easier to obtain. This is despite the fact that heroin is substantially different in its effects from those drugs.

In July 2012, the *New York Daily News* reported national data showing that overdose deaths among users between the ages of 15 and 24 had risen from 198 in 1999 to 510 in 2009. Also troubling was an 80 percent rise in teens seeking treatment for addiction, from 4,414 to 21,000 in the same ten-year period. Hard-hit regions can be found all over the United States, including the Great Lakes states and Oregon, which reported overdose rates tripling in the past decade.

Michael May, a youth outreach worker from Boston, Massachusetts, told WBUR radio in September 2010, "This summer has been very intense for heroin use…We've been

A man is shown entering a narcotic stage after ingesting heroin. Whether injected, smoked, or ingested by other means, heroin use is on the rise all over North America, especially among youth.

getting a lot of kids who, rather than a slow progression into injection drug use, have kind of jumped right in." Similar scenarios are playing out across North America.

The problem affects not only teens and other addicts but also their families, friends, and communities. Heroin addicts begin their journey for many reasons, with few of them realizing just how dangerous it really is. Heroin is one of the most addictive and deadly substances that humans can consume.

CHAPTER 2

YOUR BRAIN AND BODY ON HEROIN

Heroin's dangers arise from how it acts upon the brain and body. These dangers increase further when a person becomes tolerant of and eventually addicted to the drug. Even now, scientists and medical experts are not absolutely certain exactly why heroin affects the brain the way it does. Much has been discovered since the 1970s, however.

Heroin has slightly different effects depending on the way it is consumed. It can be ingested, smoked, inhaled or snorted, or injected into the body. Weaker forms of heroin will rarely deliver a potent high unless they are injected. Smoking or snorting heroin usually delivers a weaker high than injecting the drug. Recent strains of heroin are very strong, however, and can provide very potent highs no matter how they are ingested.

Endorphins: Regulating Pleasure and Pain

Endorphins are chemical compounds in the human body. They help relay messages from the body through the central nervous system (CNS), which includes the brain and spinal cord. Endorphins are known to regulate pain and pleasure in the body, and they affect many organ systems. Stress, pain, excitement, and other stimuli can alter endorphin levels.

Endorphins work as chemical messengers that affect the CNS's neurons—masses of cells making up the body's communication network. Neurons have receptors that endorphins fit onto. Scientists sometimes compare how endorphins work on receptors to the way that a key works in a lock. Only the right chemical structure unlocks the receptor, which then sends along the appropriate message that tells the body to reduce stress or pain or provide pleasure.

Opioids and Endorphins

Scientists in the 1970s observed how similar heroin's structure is to substances produced by the human body. They realized that heroin and similar drugs (like morphine and codeine)

mimic, or impersonate, endorphins. They artificially affect pleasure and pain relief. Researchers believe that opioids repeatedly
bind to the receptors, creating the extreme pleasure associated
with a heroin high. The body is fooled into thinking that these
substances belong there. This is why endorphins are also sometimes known as the body's "natural opiates."

When heroin enters the body, the levels of these mimicking
agents are higher than the body is used to. Usually the body
regulates endorphins and produces the right amount to react
to different situations. However, the body cannot regulate the
effects of heroin. That is why a heroin high can be so intense.
The body's natural reaction is to increase pleasure and reduce
pain. With heroin flooding the system and mimicking an endorphin rush, the body produces fewer endorphins naturally.

At the same time, the body is further confused by the flood
of foreign opioids, so it produces more receptor sites to
accommodate them. This is one reason for the vicious cycle
of heroin: the more receptors produced by the body, the more
heroin is needed to bind to those multiplying receptors, which
the brain mistakes for naturally occurring endorphins. Over
time, larger amounts of the foreign substance (heroin) are
required to obtain the same euphoric effect.

Getting High

Heroin affects the brain and body in powerful ways. New users
may be attracted to it because they are looking for a good

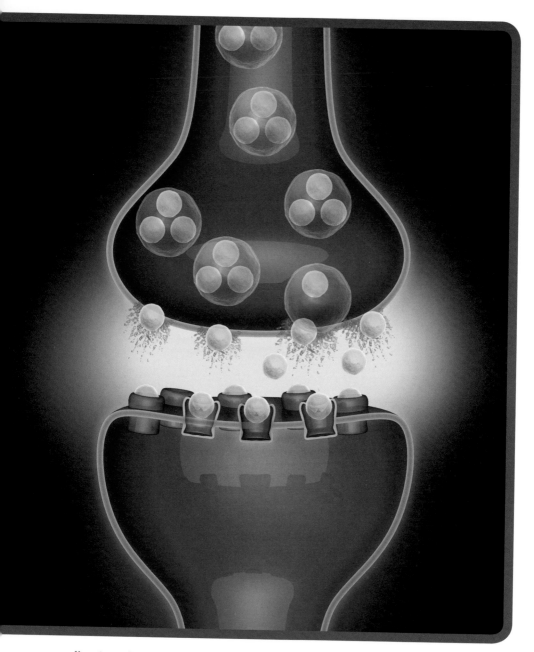

Neurotransmitters known as endorphins *(pictured in yellow)* are released from one nerve *(in blue)* across a synapse (the space between two nerves). This regulates pain and pleasure in the human body and brain.

time or because they seek escape from their own anxieties, troubles, and even physical pain.

One universal effect of heroin use is euphoria—an intense pleasure or happiness. It is most powerful in the first moments of the high, a feeling called a "rush." While scientists still debate the reason for a rush, some believe it is caused by heroin flooding the brain before it is converted into morphine.

The rush wears off after a few minutes as the drug enters the body, and a more general feeling of well-being takes over. It is described as a sensation of warmth, safety, and calmness. Some people mistake it for happiness itself. The body slows down, too, because heroin slows breathing and the heart and pulse rates.

Users also report a feeling of distance or separation from their environment. Some describe the sensation as floating. They slur their speech and become drowsy, disconnected, and inattentive. The body's movements are slowed down, making the person sluggish. Users frequently drift between wakefulness and a sleeplike state, a condition known as being "on the nod." One can nod out while lying down, sitting, standing, or even in the middle of performing a physical action. This is dangerous because users can hurt themselves and others. They also remain very vulnerable to accidents, assaults, or theft when they become oblivious to their surroundings.

First-time or novice heroin users will usually experience headaches and nausea, including vomiting, depending on the drug's potency. For many people, this is unpleasant enough to

A man is pictured nodding off after shooting heroin. The drug provides escape and pleasure but also makes users unaware of their environment, making them vulnerable to theft, violence, accidents, injury, and death.

discourage them from future use. The drug also suppresses the cough reflex, which, combined with nausea, can be dangerous for the first timer, who risks choking on his or her own vomit.

Overdose

Overdose (OD) is one of the most frightening and tragic consequences of heroin use. Anyone can OD on heroin, whether

he or she is a first-time, casual, or long-term and addicted user.
Occasional or casual users also risk their lives because their tolerance for the drug has diminished since the last time they
used. Users can OD from an unexpectedly strong dose of the
drug because it can be difficult to judge purity. Other factors,
such as the ingestion of other toxic substances, can increase the
chances of overdose. Many heroin overdoses occur while
the user is simultaneously using other drugs or alcohol.

The main causes of death during a heroin overdose are
respiratory and sometimes pulmonary failure: the user stops
breathing or his or her heart stops. Not all overdoses are fatal,
but many are. Many victims do not die quickly but instead
experience a slowdown in breathing over time. This is especially
tragic when a person could have been saved, but he or she was
either alone or surrounded by other addicts too high to
respond to or notice the emergency. If medical personnel do
not arrive in time, victims can slip into a coma or die. Even sur-
vivors may suffer brain damage or other catastrophic,
permanent health problems.

Other Physical Effects

Heroin use produces a dry, sticky feeling in the mouth. Like
other drugs and some prescription medications, heroin inter-
feres with brain messages that tell the salivary glands to
produce saliva. A user's skin may also become cold, clammy,
and pale.

The drug affects many of the automatic functions of the body and nervous system, and it slows down many of the body's processes. For this reason, another side effect for heroin users is constipation. Itchiness is also common because the drug releases histamines, which the body otherwise produces in response to infections and allergies and other stimuli, such as mosquito bites. Skin inflammation can also occur. Heroin causes the eyes' pupils to constrict, or get smaller, a phenomenon called miosis.

THE OVERDOSE "CURE"

Medical first responders and emergency room personnel have long used Narcan—the brand name of the generic drug naloxone—as the first line of defense against overdoses. When injected into a victim, the drug can reverse the most serious effects of an overdose, taking as little as a minute to revive someone and working for up to forty-five minutes. This is often enough time to get the victim to a hospital. Harm-reduction health advocates have fought to make Narcan more accessible to community institutions and even users themselves, arguing that it can save many more lives. Critics have opposed this, claiming that wider availability of Narcan will cause more reckless behavior and encourage heroin use.

Paramedics and doctors rush a patient from an ambulance into the hospital. When heroin users overdose, it's often a race against time to make sure that the victim does not die.

Addiction: A Vicious Cycle

As a person abuses heroin over time, the body's natural endorphin production is shut down. The heroin rush takes the place of normal endorphin production and the body adapts to these circumstances. This is why the habitual user, whose body is no longer producing endorphins properly, needs the drug simply to feel normal. Users report that they lose the ability to feel

A user is shown with a needle, spoon, lighter, and tourniquet, sometimes known collectively as "gear." Shooting is both the most potent and most dangerous way to take heroin.

pleasure as the body builds up its heroin tolerance. They rarely stay at the same dosage of the drug for long. Attempting to recapture that first-time high and euphoria, they are forced to take larger and larger quantities of the drug.

Gradually, addicts need greater amounts of heroin simply to avoid feeling extremely sick—that is, suffer withdrawal. The psychological toll of heroin abuse and addiction is equally frightening. Users begin to panic if they don't get the next fix quickly. This is where the vicious cycle of addiction truly picks up horrifying speed.

CHAPTER 3

HEROIN AND HEALTH: THE UGLY TRUTH

eroin's negative effects are well known, both in the short- and long-term. Its use can ruin a user's health in many ways, both directly and indirectly. In addition, the lifestyle of the user also causes secondary health effects that can be just as destructive.

In and of itself, heroin as a substance is perhaps not as destructive as drugs like methamphetamine or even alcohol. Damage to the body, its organs, and its systems does occur, however, although it is not universal among addicts. Rather, the ways in which users administer heroin, the way addicts live their daily lives, and the risks and effects of overdosing are what make it so perilous. Along with these dangers, certain side effects can cause great discomfort, even if they are not life-threatening.

Snorting and Smoking Dope

Many addicts begin using heroin by snorting (sniffing) or smoking it. Repeated, daily sniffing of any powder is bad, but exposing the nasal membranes to heroin and its cutting agents causes sinus problems and nosebleeds. Users sharing straws or rolled-up banknotes also risk spreading contagious, blood-borne diseases.

Smoking heroin—sometimes known as "chasing the dragon" or "freebasing"—is another way of ingesting the drug. This is typically done by inhaling the vapors from a heated solution of heroin. Although this has historically been a less popular method of ingestion, recent rises in heroin's potency have made the smoking of the drug more widespread. Like smoking any unnatural substance, heroin smokers risk not only addiction but also damage to the throat and lungs from prolonged use.

Needles

Many of the risks associated with heroin arise from the use of hypodermic needles—the preferred method of delivery for addicts. Users mix the drug with water and heat up the solution, which they then administer via an injection. The most common injection route, intravenous, is directly into a vein, typically in the arm. This provides the quickest rush and high. Another way is injecting the drug into the muscles, or intramuscular injection. Shooting into the skin—subcutaneous injection, also called "skin popping"—is a similar method.

Addicts will shoot heroin as often as they can into a functioning blood vein. After a while, however, these repeated injections collapse the vein. Inflammation and blood blockage make the vein useless, and the healing scar tissue causes the sides of the vein to join together. Collapsed veins are often permanent. This forces users to move on to other veins. If users run out of usable veins in their arms, they move to other parts of the body, like the legs or groin. Usually users switch to intramuscular or subcutaneous injection only if absolutely necessary, mainly because heroin takes longer to hit the system with these methods.

Needle use is dangerous regardless of the area injected. However, inexperienced users, or users who may already be too high to accurately find an injection point, run greater risks. A user may push a needle too far, popping it out the other side of the vein wall, resulting in a blown vein that spills some blood out under the skin. There is always the risk of blood loss if a user accidentally hits a larger vein or artery.

Another danger from injection is the development of an abscess. An abscess is an accumulation of pus in an inflamed area. It can be caused by a bacterial infection or other

Heroin is a dangerous drug on its own terms, but the ways in which it is ingested—by needle, smoking, or snorting—compound these dangers and further ravage the bodies of users.

foreign substance. The abscess may block blood flow and cause tissue damage. One of the worst-case scenarios if an abscess is left untreated is gangrene, a dangerous condition in which the user's flesh dies and turns green. This sometimes requires emergency surgery to amputate a limb or other affected area.

One telltale sign of addiction is track marks, the scars that users receive from injecting heroin. Users often try to hide these from other people and may wear long sleeves even in hot weather to keep their addiction a secret.

HIV/AIDS

Intravenous (IV) drug users are one of the most at-risk groups for the contraction of HIV, or human immunodeficiency virus, which causes acquired immunodeficiency syndrome (AIDS). AIDS is transmitted via bodily fluids through risky activities such as unprotected sex. It can also be spread when IV drug addicts share needles, and virus-carrying blood from an infected person comes into contact with the blood of a previously healthy user. AIDS destroys the human immune system, making the victim vulnerable to many other different illnesses and health complications.

Unless addicts obtain clean needles every time they shoot up and do not share needles with other users, they risk contracting AIDS and other debilitating or life-threatening infections. An addict going through withdrawal may not have

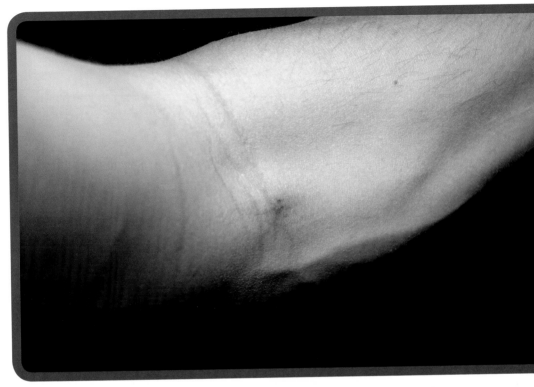

Pictured here is a wound incurred from a hypodermic needle. Needles can damage the body and serve as a means of transmitting blood-borne diseases like AIDS, hepatitis, and other contagions.

the patience to wait to get his or her hands on a clean needle, something that is not always easy to obtain.

There is no cure yet for AIDS. While modern medicine can extend a patient's life for years—even decades—many with full-blown AIDS still live under a death sentence. AIDS sufferers may have to live through severe bouts of illness and have a very poor quality of life. The wide variety of drugs they must take to treat their condition can also cause great discomfort and have unpleasant side effects.

A user shoots up in an out-of-the way place. Gathering together to engage in such risky behavior dramatically increases heroin's risks, especially if dirty needles are shared.

Hepatitis C

A disease common among heroin addicts is hepatitis C. It is a serious disease that inflames and scars the liver, causing liver failure or liver cancer if left untreated, along with other complications. Symptoms can include fatigue, itchiness, jaundice, a yellowing of the skin and whites of the eyes, and pain in the joints, stomach, and muscles. Many with hepatitis C who receive treatment experience additional suffering from side effects of the antiviral drugs they must take.

Health experts believe that hepatitis C is up to ten times more infectious than HIV for IV drug users. It can spread through cotton and other drug paraphernalia, and it can lay undetected and dormant for years, making it dangerous for those sharing needles with an unknowingly infected user.

For years, hepatitis C was thought to especially afflict older populations. Testing programs in Massachusetts, Kentucky, Ohio, and other states, however, report a sharp uptick in cases among people under the age of thirty. In Boston, for example, the Department of Public Health told WBUR radio that infections for fifteen- to twenty-five-year-olds had doubled since 2002. In many areas, heroin addicts who use needles make up a majority of new diagnoses.

Addicts craving a fix rarely think rationally about whether their fellow users are clean, nor do many go the extra mile to ensure access to clean needles or paraphernalia. Many addicts engage in risky behavior, especially while high, such as sexual activity without protection. This puts them at even greater risk for HIV and hepatitis C.

Malnutrition and Constipation

Heroin affects the digestive system directly and indirectly. For a user, all priorities besides getting heroin become secondary, including eating properly. Simultaneously, many users suffer a loss of appetite. Not eating enough or eating poorly causes malnutrition. Weight loss, a bad complexion, and a reduced ability to combat illness and the health threats that addicts typically face are only some of the grave and worrisome consequences of heroin use.

Users also suffer from constipation. Medical experts have tied the overall slowdown of body processes associated with heroin use to the specific decrease in the activity of the digestive system, including the automatic motions that move waste out of the body.

Withdrawal: A World of Pain

If an addict quits or is unable to obtain heroin, withdrawal sets in. Addicts must prepare themselves mentally and physically and expect to endure a world of pain and discomfort during the withdrawal process.

CUTTING AGENTS

Most heroin has other substances mixed in, or "cut" in. Common cutting agents include sugar, starch, powdered milk, quinine, medications, laxatives, caffeine, talcum powder, and other household substances, as well as pharmaceutical drugs. Dealers include these to increase profits. Some are chosen for their resemblance to heroin and are believed to enhance the high or counteract certain negative side effects, such as constipation.

Some users believe quinine provides a more powerful rush, but it is more often used to disguise an impure batch of heroin. Because heroin is naturally bitter, dealers can mask impurities by adding the bitter taste that accompanies quinine. The buyer is fooled into believing that the bitterness indicates that this is an especially pure batch of heroin. Quinine, however, can cause a number of problems with prolonged use, including blindness. It may also increase the chance of overdose.

In general, users can never be certain of the strength or purity of any drug they are purchasing. Cutting agents can increase the risk of blocked blood flow in the arteries, heart tissue infections, brain and liver damage, and other life-threatening dangers.

Withdrawal symptoms can begin as early as six to eight hours after the user's last fix. Many addicts report that they have experienced the worst effects from two to three days into their withdrawal, with major discomfort receding by the fourth and fifth days. However, many physical effects of withdrawal can last for weeks or months, depending on the person. The psychological effects of withdrawal (like cravings for the drug) can last for years or even an entire lifetime.

Among the most common physical withdrawal symptoms are aches and pains. Many addicts describe these as similar to the kind accompanying the flu, but more intense. Because the brain of the heroin addict is no longer producing endorphins correctly and the false euphoria supplied by heroin is now absent, the body of the addict experiencing withdrawal can't cope with the pain.

Heroin blocks pain receptors in the body. Without the drug, these receptors are exposed. When an addict goes through withdrawal, he or she must deal with a much higher than normal sensitivity to pain. Especially for those going cold turkey—quitting all at once, with no other drugs or therapies to help wean them off heroin—fear of this very unpleasant experience is one reason why addicts crave and return to heroin.

Some of the other typical withdrawal symptoms include pains in the muscles, bones, and joints. Bad stomach and muscle cramps are also common. Some addicts suffer headaches, lower

Withdrawal is a painful process, even when one has some kind of support. Kicking the habit by oneself is even more painful and lonely, especially if the user has become poor, homeless, or otherwise alienated from friends and family.

back pain, and a general feeling of illness and discomfort. These symptoms can last through the first days of the withdrawal process, yet some addicts experience them for weeks or even months after getting clean.

Just as heroin users suffer constipation while on the drug, those who kick the habit often suffer diarrhea while withdrawing. Nausea, including vomiting, is also a common withdrawal symptom, as is a loss of appetite.

MYTHS & FACTS

MYTH Only people with addictive personalities need to fear becoming hooked on heroin.

FACT Anyone who does heroin, even once, can become an addict because the drug is so powerful.

MYTH Only those who administer heroin with needles need to fear HIV and other diseases.

FACT HIV, hepatitis C, and other contagious diseases can also be spread by sharing the implements used for snorting, as well as by sexual contact.

MYTH Heroin is a relatively harmless drug because of its sedative and depressant properties, unlike the occasionally violent reactions caused by substances like alcohol or methamphetamines.

FACT Despite its calming properties, heroin addiction is often linked with the criminal activity and violence that addicts often commit to obtain money for the drug.

CHAPTER 4

THE SO-CALLED LIFE OF AN ADDICT

Many heroin addicts do not fit common stereotypes. Some people imagine addicts to be poor, possibly homeless. They are often assumed to be criminals, existing outside of society's mainstream. In reality, heroin addicts come from all backgrounds—city, suburb, and small town; rich, middle class, and poor; law-abiding citizens and criminals; and working people and the unemployed. Heroin does not discriminate when it comes to hooking users and destroying lives.

From Experimentation to Addiction

There are as many paths to heroin addiction as there are types of addicts. Initially, some simply seek a good time while partying with friends. They hope for a better high than alcohol or marijuana. Others want to escape depression, anxiety, or other emotional pain. Still others become addicted to painkillers after surgery or a sports injury. Heroin provides them a cheaper, more accessible alternative to prescription drugs.

Whatever the path to heroin addiction, the drug's powerful high soon takes over the user's life. Users make excuses and justifications, telling themselves, "Just a little bit more," or, "This time will be the last time." Few take their drug use seriously until it is too late.

For lucky first-time heroin users, the nausea and vomiting that accompany initial use are enough to scare them off forever. Many first-time users, however, are drawn back by the powerful, euphoric high. Starting with a little hit provided by friends, they soon begin buying their own supply. Recreational and weekend dabbling become more frequent. Once someone is using multiple times a day, he or she is hooked. Even in this horrible situation, users may tell themselves that everything is fine.

A Life Transformed

Heroin dramatically changes the rhythms and priorities of users' lives: getting the next hit becomes each day's overriding objective. They keep their drug use a secret because concerned family and friends are a threat to getting high. Life becomes a high-stakes game of achieving that high while somehow hiding it from parents, siblings, teachers, and law enforcement. Even friends may be out of the loop or dropped in favor of loyalty to the addiction. Addicts risk expulsion from school, punishment by the justice system, and the embarrassment and shame of their relatives and peers.

It may be easy to hide addiction at first. As addicts begin to need more of the drug, however, they find it harder to continue normal routines, until they cannot function normally at all. Being high in school, at work, or at home makes them stick out like a sore thumb. Rather than seek help to kick the habit, the addict starts failing at school or ditches classes altogether. Addicts lose their jobs because they don't show up or cannot function at work.

Heroin quickly strains friendships and other relationships. Friends may be concerned and try to help. The power of addiction is often too strong, and addicts often turn away from even their best friends. As their behavior becomes increasingly odd, selfish, and unattractive, their friends begin to turn away from them, too.

Addicts find refuge in codependent friendships with other addicts in which they enable, support, and excuse or encourage each other's drug use. Even these false friendships may not last long, however. The longer someone is addicted, the more likely he or she and his or her fellow addicts will lie, cheat, and steal. They will betray each other to feed their drug habit.

Addiction means that nothing else matters more than the drug. Users lose sight of everything else of value in their lives and can often focus only on the daily struggle of scoring the drug.

Alienation from Family

Addicts often have strained relationships with family members. The longer addiction continues, the less parents and others will trust an addict—even their own flesh and blood—to do the right thing. Some parents may be very strict and threaten to report their child to the authorities or kick them out of the house. They may be unable to think of another solution that will save their child from a likely death from overdose, a

Heroin users may eventually burn all the bridges in their lives, leaving them alone and wracked with guilt, anxiety, despair, and depression.

criminal lifestyle, HIV infection, or any of heroin's many other life-threatening risks.

A Life of Crime

Addicts fool themselves into believing that they can be high-functioning users. The more heroin they need to feel the high they used to experience, or even just to avoid feeling sick, the more money they need. Because it is difficult to hold a job while on heroin, addicts borrow money from others and usually wipe out their savings. Some sell off their possessions. They get on the all-too-predictable road that many addicts find themselves on: a life of crime.

Theft from one's parents or other family members is just the beginning. Other crimes that addicts commonly commit include shoplifting, burglary, auto theft, and other dangerous activities. They risk not only a prison sentence or other punishments but also serious bodily harm. They may even get killed in

Petty theft can escalate to more serious crimes with full-blown addiction. Even good people can enter a life of crime to fund their drug habit.

the process of committing a crime. Sadly, the prospect of withdrawal and living without heroin makes nearly any risk acceptable to an addict.

Hitting Bottom

An addict who is kicked out of his or her home, and who fails to get clean despite rehab or other means, may end up homeless or crashing with addicts and other criminals. Many junkies turn to selling heroin themselves in order to support their habit. Still others (both male and female) turn to prostitution. Selling their bodies makes them vulnerable to disease, destroys their self-esteem, and exposes them to violent and unethical sexual predators.

Every day a junkie wakes up sick, he or she must hatch a new scheme to get dope, stay alive, and stay one step ahead of the police. The addict may also face a day-to-day existence in an unpredictable, criminal underworld. Because judgment is clouded by the overwhelming need for the drug, the addict may underestimate or ignore the risks inherent in stealing from or taking advantage of dealers and other dangerous criminals.

Hunger, homelessness, and disease are some of the other troubles that addicts face all too often. Such problems are bad enough in isolation without adding drug addiction to the mix. Taken all together, it is easy to see why many users describe addiction as akin to losing their souls.

NEVER QUITE FREE: RUSSELL BRAND

Actor, musician, and comedian Russell Brand has been honest with his fans and the public about something many celebrities would rather keep secret: his former life as a heroin addict. In an essay he wrote for the British newspaper the *Spectator*, he admitted that he is constantly reminded of his need for heroin, even though he has been clean for years. His daily battle might be triggered whenever he faces any problem in his life, however big or small, or even when he visits places or sees people whom he associates with heroin use. He admits it is difficult but worthwhile to stay clean, adding that the good life he now enjoys comes with a price: "The price of this is constant vigilance because the disease of addiction is not rational."

Hitting bottom can mean becoming homeless or even worse fates. Bottoming-out is often the only thing that convinces many users to finally get clean.

An Important Life Decision

Before taking heroin, teens should ask themselves a serious question: is it really worth it? They should consider all the things that they enjoy and that make life worth living: home, family, friends, hobbies, work, school, real emotional connections, and more. Doing heroin even once is like tossing a coin to see whether to trade all those things, including life itself, for an artificial high that soon fades and the host of horrors it ushers in. These very real horrors include dissociation, alienation, unemployment, poverty, homelessness, disease, and death. Any high that invites these profound lows into your life is clearly not the euphoric experience that you will expect it to be.

5

GETTING CLEAN

Deciding to kick heroin addiction is the most important step a person can take. Some users are forced to by circumstances. They may end up in jail or be required to enter a treatment program instead of facing prison time. Others quit because they have hit rock bottom, experiencing the most miserable depths of addiction. An overdose or the death of a friend, relative, companion, or spouse may serve as a wake-up call to quit. The decision to quit might be difficult, but following through can be just as hard.

Detox

Detoxification—detox, for short—is the process of removing heroin completely from your system. It is the most basic route to quitting. One detox strategy is to limit and decrease the amount of heroin taken over time, eventually quitting altogether. Quitting abruptly, or going cold turkey, is usually recognized as more common and effective, at least in the short term. Both methods carry with them the unpleasant side effects of withdrawal, however.

Gradual weaning from the drug and cold turkey are both do-it-yourself methods. They do not require checking into a private or public treatment program. Yet these methods require the kind of discipline that many addicts lack, and the withdrawal process is not safely overseen by trained doctors, mental health counselors, or other health care professionals. Simply quitting without professional treatment and therapy often leads to relapse and medical emergencies. Heroin cravings can remain, while the many problems, stresses, and triggers that addicts struggle with—and that led to addiction in the first place—remain unaddressed.

Anti-Addictive Drugs

Detox is only the first step in effective treatment for heroin addiction. Considering that many addicts fear withdrawal sickness, most seek detoxification and further treatment that includes the use of anti-addictive drugs. These are substances that are used to satisfy the addict's urge for heroin but do not have narcotic effects.

Among the most widely used of these is methadone, which is administered in programs all around the world. A typical dose of methadone greatly eases heroin withdrawal symptoms for a period of about twenty-four hours. The size of the dose depends on the user. Too large an amount can cause intoxication and even overdose, while too little may be ineffective. A proper dosage does not interfere with normal, everyday activities. It works by reducing the need for heroin, but it also lingers in the body longer than heroin does.

Methadone is only administered by medical professionals as part of a treatment program. It is usually taken orally once a day. Many patients become addicted to methadone itself, and weaning a user off of it also requires professional care. A user may stay on methadone for weeks or months, with dosages decreasing over time until he or she is able to live normally without it. In some cases, addicts may remain on methadone for years, especially if they find it difficult to control their heroin cravings even after a long period of treatment.

Discontinuing methadone treatment can be as difficult for some users as quitting heroin in the first place. Its withdrawal symptoms can include abdominal cramps, insomnia, diarrhea, nausea and vomiting, and acute pain, among other side effects. In addition, methadone has its own unique side effects that differ widely among patients. These may include dryness of the mouth and skin, nausea and vomiting, mild disorientation, blurred vision, constipation, vertigo or dizziness, and other symptoms. For a small percentage of patients who are allergic

Registered nurse Mary Sinden watches a client of the ARTS Outpatient Clinic in Denver, Colorado, take a dose of methadone.

to methadone, dangerous side effects can include breathing trouble or respiratory arrest, trouble urinating, fainting spells, cold flashes, and intense anxiety.

Other Drugs

Other drugs can serve as substitutes for methadone, help supplement it, or ease the user's transition away from it.

Buprenorphine, known commercially as Subutex and Suboxone, is less potent and addictive than methadone. It is less likely to result in overdose and causes fewer withdrawal symptoms. Unlike methadone, it is available by prescription from some doctors. Not all patients respond to it, however, and it is prescribed for long-term use. Quitting the drug must be managed carefully because it can cause potentially serious withdrawal symptoms and complications.

Naltrexone, prescribed for opiates and alcoholism, can be taken by tablet daily or periodically throughout the week. Naltrexone works by blocking the effects of opiates. However, it does not alleviate withdrawal symptoms and is not recommended for users who have recently kicked the habit.

Inpatients and Outpatients

Treatment programs can be divided into two types: inpatient and outpatient treatment. Addicts entering inpatient programs submit to detoxification and treatment by entering a hospital or residential treatment facility. This means living on-site with other recovering addicts while undergoing more intense treatment, as well as individual and group therapy. Inpatient programs typically last anywhere from twenty-eight days to several months. Some even extend as long as a year or more, depending on how badly at-risk for relapse an addict is.

There are many different types of inpatient programs. Some are public, state-mandated ones. They are geared toward addicts who have left the prison system after serving sentences for drug possession or other drug-related crimes. Some require that addicts remain on-site all the time. Others allow their patients to find work or perform other activities in the outside world as long as they return to the facility before a mandatory curfew. Other treatment centers are private and are paid for by an addict or someone else, like a parent or relative. Some of the private treatment centers that cater to wealthier clients can almost seem like vacation resorts or boarding schools. No matter how welcoming or cozy their treatment environment is, however, patients must remember that they are there to

RAPID OPIATE DETOXIFICATION (ROD)

One controversial detoxification process involves using drugs like naltrexone and even naloxone (the "overdose cure") for something called rapid opiate detoxification, or ROD. These drugs are combined with the use of anesthesia, which lessens painful withdrawal symptoms. Addicts are attracted to this option because it can provide a much quicker detox process. However, many medical professionals believe ROD to be dangerous, claiming that some patients have died as a result of the method. They consider it an unrealistic "magic bullet" that delivers short-term results but does nothing to prevent those with addictive personalities from seeking replacements for their heroin addiction, like alcohol or other drugs. Addicts can trick themselves into believing that they need not put in the hard physical, mental, and emotional work of true recovery.

recover and develop the personal tools they need once released to stay off heroin. Inpatient programs exist for users who need more help and supervision because they are at greater risk of using again.

Outpatient programs are more flexible. Patients live on their own while visiting a clinic. They attend therapy sessions and other appointments, often while taking an anti-addictive drug like methadone. Many outpatient programs are run by city, county, or state governments and require methadone treatment and periodic drug tests. Outpatients can work, go to school, and generally go about their everyday lives. Many inpatients transfer into outpatient programs, especially if they make progress and require less supervision.

Whichever route an addict takes (or is required to take) is based on individual needs. The important thing is that each person is matched to the level of care that he or she needs and that will best aid him or her in kicking heroin once and for all.

Narcotics Anonymous and Other Support Groups

One organization fighting addiction is the international self-help recovery community known as Narcotics Anonymous (NA). NA guides recovering addicts through a process in which they gain strength by admitting their mistakes, doing their best to gain forgiveness from others, and supporting and relying upon

Addict James Reyes shares his story during group therapy in Sacramento, California. Reyes was lucky to enter treatment rather than going to jail for a low-level drug offense, thereby dodging the fate of many of his peers.

each other. NA holds regular, daily meetings that are open to all addicts and those who fear they are addicted. It has chapters in more than 131 nations.

Other support groups include SMART Recovery and the Secular Organization for Sobriety/Save Our Selves (SOS). Along with NA and other twelve-step organizations, these groups encourage addicts to share their stories. They emphasize recovery as a continuing, lifelong process. Addicts may also seek aid from community organizations, church groups and clergy, and private psychologists or therapists.

Major Changes

Without making crucial changes to his or her lifestyle, group of friends, and perspective, the addict remains vulnerable to relapsing. Treatment professionals, therapists, and concerned family and friends all stress this important component of recovery.

Addicts must watch the company they keep, avoiding ties with the drug and party lifestyle, including contact with other addicts and dealers. This includes even those people with whom they were formerly very close. At the same time, they should strengthen ties with drug-free friends and take part in other, more positive pursuits. These include satisfying hobbies, sports, or other activities that connect them with supportive friends and positive role models. Clubs, church, community involvement, and family ties can all help someone struggling with sobriety.

The same goes for teens seeking to stay clean. As tough as it may seem at first, they need to avoid school cliques or other social settings known for drug or alcohol use. While this may not be possible all the time, it is especially important to make the effort in the first months after initial recovery. Avoiding places where drug activity occurs—whether that means a

Danny DiPascale, forty-seven, from Malden, Massachusetts, is shown here after finishing treatment. An addict since age sixteen, DiPascale spent seven years in federal prison.

particular place at school (like the parking lot, under the bleachers, or in the adjacent woods) or a specific part of town or certain people's homes—is also essential.

The Change Within

Equally important for addicts is making profound changes within themselves. All the treatment, therapy, and special precautions mean little if someone lacks the strength of character to stay clean or if the need to get high remains too powerful to resist. This includes seeking help from outside parties for problems such as depression, self-loathing, anxiety, and other serious psychological problems.

Experiencing sadness, feeling excluded, being overwhelmed by life, and dealing with trouble at school or at home are natural and common parts of growing up. For many teens, these are the reasons why they turn to drugs in the first place. If someone is at risk, it is that much more vital they get the help they

Finding ways to feel good about oneself, whether it comes in the form of exercise, work, creative outlets, or other life-affirming pursuits, is crucial to the detox and recovery process.

need. They must develop the strength—inside themselves and among a support network of friends, family, and counseling and medical professionals—to stay clean.

In the long-term, addicts must be ever vigilant. Rather than run from their emotions and life's difficulties, they must make the tough decision to face them head on. This will require great courage, determination, and steadfastness. Doing this, they can emerge from the process more self-aware, finding happiness in themselves and the world around them. Otherwise, heroin will remain a temptation that will almost certainly prove deadly.

TEN GREAT QUESTIONS TO ASK A DRUG COUNSELOR

1. What exactly makes heroin so addictive?

2. Can someone remain a casual or occasional user and be OK?

3. Are smoking or snorting heroin safer than injecting it?

4. Is there a cure for heroin addiction?

5. Why do addicts fear withdrawal so much?

6. Why are heroin addicts considered untrustworthy?

7. What are some of heroin's gateway drugs?

8. How does too much heroin cause an overdose?

9. What are the dangers of using needles?

10. What drugs are used in heroin detoxification and treatment?

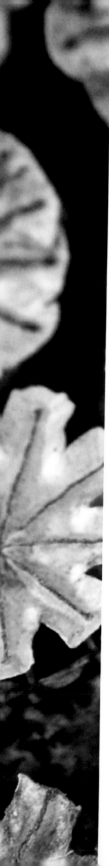

GLOSSARY

cold turkey Quitting heroin or another drug abruptly, often accompanied by painful withdrawal symptoms.

cutting agent A substance that is mixed in with pure heroin.

endorphins Chemical compounds in the human body that help regulate pain and pleasure; sometimes called the body's "natural opiates."

inpatient treatment Intensive drug treatment in which the patient resides at the site of treatment in a therapeutic community.

intramuscular Through the muscle; addicts may inject heroin intramuscularly, or directly into muscle tissue.

intravenous Through the vein; addicts often inject heroin intravenously, or directly into a vein.

junk A slang term for heroin.

junkie A slang term for a heroin addict.

opiate A drug naturally derived from the opium poppy plant.

opioid A natural or synthetic drug that has properties similar to heroin.

opium An opiate paste, usually smoked, which is one of the oldest drugs known to humankind.

opium poppy The plant from which opium, heroin, morphine, and other opiates and opioids are derived.

outpatient treatment A treatment program in which a person lives on his or her own while recovering from addiction.

FOR MORE INFORMATION

Narcotics Anonymous (NA)
P.O. Box 9999
Van Nuys, CA 91409
(818) 773-9999
Web site: http://www.na.org
Narcotics Anonymous is the largest international
  twelve-step program serving as a supportive com-
  munity for those recovering from drug addiction.

National Association of Addiction Treatment Providers
  (NAATP)
11380 Prosperity Farms Road, Suite 209A
Palm Beach Gardens, FL 33410
(561) 429-4527
Web site: https://www.naatp.org
The NAATP is an organization comprised of many different substance abuse treatment programs and
  groups, providing leadership, advocacy, and support
  services to members.

National Institute on Drug Abuse (NIDA)
6001 Executive Boulevard
Room 5213, MSC 9561
Bethesda, MD 20892
(301) 443-1124
Web site: http://www.drugabuse.gov

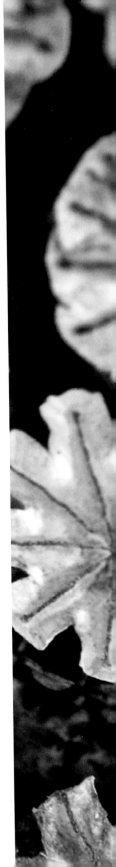

The National Institute on Drug Abuse, part of the National
   Institutes of Health, under the U.S. Department of Health
   and Human Services, is one of the largest organizations to
   research addiction, drug use trends, and drug treatment.

SMART Recovery Canada
223 12 Avenue SW
Calgary, AB T2R 0G9
Canada
(403) 619-4210
Web site: http://www.smartrecovery.ca
SMART Recovery Canada runs a free, self-help program dedi-
   cated to addiction recovery.

Web Sites

Due to the changing nature of Internet links, Rosen Publishing
has developed an online list of Web sites related to the subject
of this book. This site is updated regularly. Please use this link to
access the list:

http://www.rosenlinks.com/DAC/Heroi

FOR FURTHER READING

Brezina, Corona. *Heroin: The Deadly Addiction* (Drug Abuse and Society). New York, NY: Rosen Publishing Group, 2009.

Burgess, Melvin. *Smack*. New York, NY: Square Fish Books, 2010.

Carlson, Hannah. *Addiction: The Brain Disease*. Branford, CT: Bick Publishing, 2010.

Higgins, Melissa. *Living with Substance Addiction* (Living with Health Challenges). Edina, MN: Essential Library/ABDO, 2012.

Kuhar, Michael J. *Substance Abuse, Addiction, and Treatment*. Tarrytown, NY: Marshall Cavendish, 2011.

O'Toole, Julie. *Heroin*. London, England: Turnaround, 2008.

Sanna, E. J. *Heroin and Other Opioids: Poppies' Perilous Children* (Illicit and Misused Drugs). Broomall, PA: Mason Crest Publishers, 2012.

Shantz-Hilkes, Chloe, ed. *Hooked: When Addiction Hits Home*. Toronto, ON, Canada: Annick Press, 2013.

Sheff, Nic. *We All Fall Down: Living with Addiction*. New York, NY: Little, Brown Books for Young Readers, 2012.

Walker, Ida. *Addiction in America: Society, Psychology, and Heredity* (Illicit and Misused Drugs). Broomall, PA: Mason Crest Publishers, 2012.

Walker, Ida. *Addiction Treatment: Escaping the Trap* (Illicit and Misused Drugs). Broomall, PA: Mason Crest Publishers, 2012.

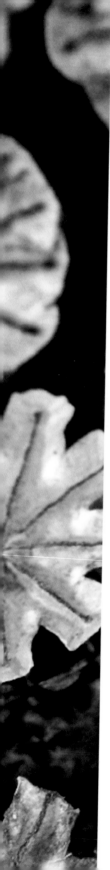

BIBLIOGRAPHY

Bebinger, Martha. "Hepatitis C Spikes Among Young Heroin Users." WBUR.org, September 9, 2010. Retrieved March 2, 2013 (http://www.wbur.org/2010/09/09/hep-c).

Brand, Russell. "I Thought About Taking Heroin Yesterday." *The Sun*, March 6, 2013. Retrieved March 15, 2013 (http://www.thesun.co.uk/sol/homepage/showbiz/4826765/russell-brand-i-thought-about-taking-heroin-again.html).

Farrell, Michael B. "Heroin's Comeback: Busts at Levels Not Seen Since the '70s." *Christian Science Monitor*, August 5, 2009. Retrieved January 28, 2013 (http://www.csmonitor.com/USA/Society/2009/0805/p02s07-ussc.html).

Horng, Eric. "Heroin Use a Growing Problem in Chicago Area." ABC 7 News Chicago, March 9, 2013. Retrieved March 13, 2013 (http://abclocal.go.com/wls/story?section=news/local&id=9021726).

Moore, Molly, and Douglas Farah. "Mexican Heroin on Rise in U.S." *Washington Post*, June 2, 1998. Retrieved January 29, 2013 (http://www.washingtonpost.com/wp-srv/inatl/longterm/drugs).

Robson, Philip. *Forbidden Drugs*. Oxford, UK: Oxford University Press, 2002.

Sotonoff, Jamie. "Suburban Heroin Problem Called 'a Medical Emergency.'" *Chicago Daily Herald*, March 11, 2013. Retrieved March 20, 2013 (http://www.dailyherald.com/article/20130311/news/703119782).

INDEX

A

addiction, 6, 14, 15, 23–25, 30, 34–36, 37, 46
anti-addictive drugs, 47–49, 52

B

Brand, Russell, 44

C

crime, and heroin, 4, 42–44

D

detox, 47, 50
diseases, 6, 12, 30–33, 37

E

endorphins, 16–17, 23, 35

F

family, alienation from, 41–42

G

getting clean, 46–56

H

hepatitis C, 6, 32–33, 37
heroin
   dangers of, 4, 6, 13–14, 19, 20–21, 26–36, 37, 40, 45
   effects on body and brain, 15–25, 26, 27, 33, 35
   getting clean, 46–56
   history of, 8–10
   and hitting bottom, 43–44, 46
   myths and facts about, 37
HIV/AIDS, 6, 12, 30–31, 32, 33, 37, 42

M

methadone, 48–50, 52

N

naloxone (Narcan), 22, 51
Narcotics Anonymous, 52–53
needles, and heroin injection, 11, 15–16, 27–31, 32, 33, 37

O

opioids, 7–8, 16–17
opium, 7, 8–9, 10
overdoses, 13, 20–21, 22, 27, 34, 46, 48, 50

P

poppy cultivation, 10

R

rapid opiate detoxification, 51

S

smoking heroin, 11–12, 15–16, 27
snorting heroin, 11–12, 15–16, 27, 37
support groups, 52–54

T

teens, and heroin, 4, 6, 11–13, 54–55
therapy, 50, 52, 55, 56
treatment programs, 43, 46, 47, 48–52

W

withdrawal, 25, 30–31, 34–36, 43, 47, 48, 50, 51

About the Author

Philip Wolny is a writer from Queens, New York. His other substance abuse–related title for Rosen Publishing is *Abusing Prescription Drugs* (Incredibly Disgusting Drugs).

Photo Credits

Cover, p. 1 Vladimir Wrangel/Shutterstock. com; p. 5 iStockphoto.com/Thinkstock; pp. 7, 15, 26, 38, 46 © iStockphoto.com/Fyletto; p. 8 Scott Nelson/Getty Images; p. 11 U.S. DEA; p. 14 Doug Menuez/Photodisc/Getty Images; p. 18 Claus Lunau/Science Source; p. 20 Andy Bullock/The Image Bank/Getty Images; pp. 23, 43 Monkey Business Images/Shutterstock.com; p. 24 Ingrid W./Shutterstock.com; p. 29 Steve Allen/Brand X Pictures/Getty Images; p. 31 Damian Herde/Shutterstock.com; p. 32 Evgeny Atamanenko/Shutterstock.com; p. 36 Andrea Zanchi/Vetta/Getty Images; p. 41 Artem Furman/Shutterstock.com; p. 42 Elena Rostunova/Shutterstock.com; p. 45 Mike Cherim/Vetta/Getty Images; p. 49 Brian Brainerd/Denver Post/Getty Images; pp. 53, 55 © AP Images; p. 56 Luti/Shutterstock. com; pp. 58, 60, 62, 63, 64 © iStockphoto.com/egiss.

Designer: Michael Moy; Photo Researcher: Marty Levick